Wisconsin River of Grace

wisconsin
river of grace

Kyle L. White

Cornerstone Press
University of Wisconsin-Stevens Point

Cornerstone Press
University of Wisconsin-Stevens Point
Stevens Point, WI

www.uwsp.edu/english/cornerstone

Printed in the United States of America

Library of Congress Control Number: 2009938271

Lyrics from "Sad, Lonely, Rotten World" (*Portrait of Narcissus*, Fundamental Records, 2006) reprinted by permission of David Wolfenberger.

Lyrics from "Ordinary Extraordinary Day" (*Mr. Buechner's Dream*, Stunt Records, 2001) reprinted by permission of Terry Scott Taylor.

ISBN: 978-0-9774802-72

The illustrations in this book were done in pen and ink with an ink wash.

For Barb, Maddie, & Keegan.

There [is]… a kind of nostalgic wildness in its name:
Wisconsin.
—August Derleth, *The Wisconsin: River of a Thousand Isles*, 1942

Men are like plants; the goodness and flavour of the fruit proceeds from the peculiar soil and exposition in which they grow.
—J. Hector St. Jean de Crevecoeur,
Letters from an American Farmer, 1782

Contents

Cold: Winter

Getting Warmer: Spring

Hot: Summer

Getting Colder: Autumn

Contents

COLD: Winter

The Dead, of Winter

Behold; hope has frozen over.

Hark; life has drawn her last bitter breath.

Come; bid a cold farewell to joy.

Winter wonderland has turned to icy wasteland.

Alas, it is over. *Sniff.*

This great and glorious Winter Sabbath has come to an end. The culmination of all things—Christmas Break across Community Unit School District #427—ends with a whimper on this dark, frigid Sunday night.

And a faint sucking noise.

At this very moment, the marrow is being drained from our children's bones. Monday morning is a mocking specter. The Ghost of Christmas-That-Didn't-Last.

The Christmas decorations have all been laid to rest, buried with the other boxes in the basement vault. And you, O Christmas tree, O Christmas tree: what did you ever do to deserve this? To be dressed up as if by a drunken undertaker. Then, to be stripped naked and thrown out the back door to shrink in the arctic air. You, O Christmas tree, who never gave up as much as one needle. You, who drank water, God bless you, like an out-of-control diabetic. You, who were at once both Frasier and fir. You, who were worth all twenty-nine dollars and ninety-nine cents. Plus the tax. God rest your soul.

And, Monday morning comes, like a slow-motion winter pileup on I-90.

Sliding.

Braking.

Sliding.

2

Braking.

Sliding.

Breaking. There is nothing we motorists can do.

It. Is. Inevitable. Bewildered victims everywhere.

"I can't do it. It's too hard. It's too-o-o hard," moans our boy as he rises up from under his covers. A resurrection into the old life.

"But, I want to keep sleeping. Five more minutes," pleads our girl.

We have passed over to the other side. That purgatory between Christmas and spring. Where the streets are paved with slush. Where we are robed in wet socks, post-nasal drippings, and Vicks VapoRub. Where every tribe and tongue and nation clears their strep throats and croaks their winter croak:

"Who will deliver us? From whence does our help come?"

Draw near, St. Casimir Pulaski—whoever you are—with your curious Monday holiday. Save us! We need you now more than ever. Mount up one more revolution. Make war against this darkness. Against the oppressive Superintendent of Schools and his minions. Dethrone him for one more day.

(And, if it is not too much to ask, a snow day on the preceding Friday. Or the following Tuesday.)

Lord, hear our prayers. Amen. And, amen.

Wisconsin is Grace

Wisconsin is grace. One of those bridges to the Divine. I don't simply mean—as some outsiders view it—the PackerCheeseBeer&Brat Cult. Which may be more of a sect, or even a denomination, if you give it, well, grace. But, I mean a genuine gift of God.

My family and I recently had lunch with some friends from L.A., who talked about the Disneyland exhibit called "California." And, they speculated, "What other state could have its own Disney attraction? Like, for instance, who would go to a Wisconsin themed park?!" Ha. Ha. Ha. But, in the front pew of my heart, I raised my hand. Hey, it's Wisconsin. My birth home. And the home of my re-birth. Because now that I live in Illinois, when I cross back over the border into God's Country, I tell people there is a sigh of relief. A burden lifted.

But, whether it's Madison, or Baraboo, Ephraim, Wisconsin Rapids, or Stevens Point, I could offer you dozens of mental snapshots of Wisconsin, where the light of grace rests just so. Like this Polaroid peel-away photo which has been framed ever-so-slightly by my revisionist history. "Mythologized," my brother says. But, we both remember. It's from when I was in kindergarten. I'm the round kid on the left…

"We don't like it here and we don't like you, Mom," we had charged matter-of-factly.

We were rebelling against an oppressive regime. Who would've believed it was possible there in central Wisconsin? Right there under the very noses of the good people of Stevens Point even? We'd had enough of work camp. Enough of sweat shop. Enough of dictatorship. There would be no more cleaning of our rooms. No more gagging from wadding paper towel to extract teepee piles of dog poop from our brown shag carpet. "Why is it my job? I didn't do it!"

My brother led the rebellion. He was nine. Four years older and wiser. He knew what was really going on around there: Stalin, Mussolini, Our Mother. We, the proletariat, stood in defiance with our rubber boots, snowmobile suits, and Green Bay Packer stocking caps. Our rebel plan? We went for the heart. "We're running away!"

4

"Where?" she asked.

"Anywhere but here," we said.

6:00 p.m. Freedom! We scuffed and shuffled down Torun Road. A dark night. Winter in Wisconsin. Our cheeks were stinging hot, as kamikaze snowflakes dive-bombed our frozen eyelashes. But it was the right thing to do.

6:06 p.m. We had walked for hours. But there we were, stalled in our tracks. We had come to that particular spot in the road. On one side, that abandoned gray house. Weathered. Windows broken. Every kid for eight blocks knew it was haunted. On the other side, my brother remembered, "There was a logging road, and it made that whole place seem like a black hole that you would get sucked into, and never come back." We didn't dare walk past it in the daylight, much less on that dreadful night.

"I ain't walkin' past it," he said.

"Me neither. Maybe we should go back," I said.

"Home?! No way!"

We looked back toward where we had made our escape, through the smudge of swarming snowflakes and blurred streetlights. A double take. A figure in the gray distance. We squinted through the dark, through the wet snow. It was coming closer. Someone. Carrying something. A club, in its right hand. Oh yes, it was a club all right! Some cartoon caveman, chicken drumstick club!

We were trapped. January sweat. Feet frozen by fear. We shivered between lurking ghosts and a madman stepping up to deliver the Stormin' Gorman Thomas homerun blow. Crack! Over the fence, into the ditch, laying us out like two deep-freeze Ball Park Franks. But, our eyes strained through the dark to capture our winter assailant. The last image we would ever see before…

"Mom? Is that you?"

(Or, maybe it was like that scratch-and-pop LP at home, where Hans

5

Christian Andersen's Little Match Girl had only enough light to show her just what she *didn't* have before she froze to death. Who gives their kids that record?)

But, no, it was Mom. And, she was carrying two scarves in her right hand.

"Why don't you come back home? We're having Polish sausage for dinner," she offered.

And this is what came out of our mouths: "Okay, Mom." *Okay, Mom.* Like it was our bright idea. And we headed for the porch light of home. Rescued. And, just like that, ghosts and fear melted like snowflakes in the hand. There was never a word mentioned about our rebel offense. It was grace. Grace wrapped in Polish sausage and applesauce.

And, our gospel reading that night was from St. Luke, chapter 15: "But while they were still a long way off, they were spotted and compassion was poured out upon them. Footsteps broke into hot pursuit of them. An embrace and kisses all around. 'Bring out the best scarves and put them on them. And put those mittens-on-a-string on their hands. And warm boots on their feet. Don't forget the plastic bread bag liners to keep those feet dry. And bring the fatted Polish sausage. Let us eat and be merry, for these sons of mine were lost and now they have been found.'" Amen.

And, amen. Wisconsin is grace.

Speed Bumps for Glaciers

It was the year of the speed bump. The year my family ran me over. Twice. I was five or six, I think. But, I'm always five or six in my revisionist history.

The first incident: Stevens Point. Central Wisconsin winter. Pre-Greenhouse Effect. Back when snow was proud. I stood on a glorious pile that was forty feet high. One of those towers created at the end of our driveway by the thundering snow plows. Mom, my brother, and sister were returning from the Thrifty-Mart with groceries, down the salt-white road in our cavernous, margarine-yellow tub of a station wagon. I slid down the snow bank and began to run alongside the car. I waved to my brother and sister, chugging white breath. They waved back. Me, in my blue-black snowmobile suit, Packer stocking cap, and faux-leather rubber boots, laughing. And, at that point, I grabbed the back door handle. My family kept waving, waving, waving, as I slipped, slipped, slipped, disappearing under the back tire. Thump. Thump. The lumbering wagon rolled over my legs and I was pressed into a stunned, fallen snow angel mold at the end of the driveway. Hot tears and breath flowed. It was an accident, I'm sure. "No broken bones," Dr. Sevenich said.

The second incident: Stevens Point. Central Wisconsin summer. Greenhouse humidity. There in the twilight, as we three siblings played in our mosquito-preserve front yard, under the tree where we had flung my sister's Barbie doll. Her neck tied to a shoe string (the Barbie's, not my sister's). My brother chased me on that red bike with the sparkly yellow banana seat and knobby tires. The five-foot orange safety flag wagging and taunting, as I laughed and panted. Barefoot, I slipped on the dewy grass. Thump. Thump. He ran over my head. Tears and sweat mingled with the fresh tread mark across my face. It was an accident. "Nothing broken," Dr. Sevenich said.

If only I had been old enough to see the conspiracy. They rolled me out like Silly Putty. Pressed and impressed. Being careful not to get any of it on the orange shag carpeting in the living room. And, in all of that formative rolling and shaping that took place in Wisconsin, I picked up pieces and bits that are now part of me.

Like the time in Wisconsin Rapids, at my grandpa and grandma's house, when I plummeted out of that tree, landing hard on my back amid the sand, pine needles, and roots. Luckily, my grandma called her doctor neighbor to come over and examine my spine. Dr. Fleming was an optometrist, but it made me feel better, I guess.

Or the time in Junction City, during one of my dad's softball games, where another kid and I thought up the clever pastime of "Rock Fight." The rules, in case you want to play at home, are simple: (1) choose a rock and a partner; (2) mark-off about ten yards between the two of you; (3) take turns throwing your rock 'til you hit your partner; and (4) first one to strike his target, wins. I wound up, pitched my rock, and missed. Wide right. The other kid, who somehow found an Indian arrowhead in the Golden Sands of Plover, fired, and in Super Slo-Mo, the projectile flew, finding its mark directly between my eyes.

Cue the deluge of blood.

And, continuing in Super Slo-Mo, I fell backward to the earth in a cloud of dust. The game announcer, over the PA, proclaimed, "Game delay! Don White, your kid is bleeding in the dirt behind the outfield fence." The softball fans *booed.*

"The beer stand is still open," came the next announcement. *Yay!*

It's been over thirty years since the stitches were removed, but I'd still punch that kid in the mouth if I saw him on the street today. I still have the scar. And, I still have the scars from rafting on the Wolf River during a storm in junior high, where my larger partner fell out the back of our yellow raft going over Boy Scout Falls. The ballast being gone, I was catapulted into the river, where my right leg wrenched and wedged between two underwater rocks. I was held down there, steeped in a cloud of bubbles, pressed by the current, filling up on the Wolf, but somehow found myself puking up water on the river bank. It's the closest I've ever come to biting the dust. Fittingly, it almost happened at the hands of Wisconsin's geology.

Considering all this, I realize I have an embarrassing number of stories of run-ins with Wisconsin soil. A veritable state tour, including: the Kettle Moraine, while mountain biking; the smooth white rocks of Washington Island; the sand beach of Pine Lake in Westfield; the gravel on the shoulders of the roads of Amherst. You name the region; I have a story best left for another time.

And, while at first read, this appears to be a history of my maladroit life—an outward demonstration of the rocks in my head—it is, below surface, a testimonial of the irresistible, gravitational pull of Wisconsin. God's Country. Part of the conspiracy. All those times spent lying flat on my back in the rich soil of this state, I should've looked up, and looked around, at the grace of my surroundings. I should've seen the clues, but I finally get it now, after moving away. I am a human glacier tripping and stumbling and sliding through this beautiful state, picking up bits and pieces wherever I go. All magnetic fragments that point True North.

Now that I get it, I no longer fight the pull of this place. Wisconsin, for me, has become reorientation and grace. And, my brother still tells the stories of the year I was run over by my family, pressed into the dirt. He still tells the stories of the rock to my head and the rocks in my head. Still making and revising our history. And, still, I am being smoothed, shaped, and polished in the rock tumbler of Wisconsin. But no need to call Dr. Sevenich, God rest his soul, I get it now.

Grandfather Christmas

We always had to wait. After dinner. After the dishes were done. After dessert. And, after singing. You, Grandpa, with your plentitude of slicked back hair and your gray cardigan sweater, pumping away at the console organ. Your hands flowing back and forth across that glorious machine like a conjuring magician. "Santa Claus is Coming to Town" with the castanets tab engaged. And, "Rudolph the Red-Nosed Reindeer" with marimba and your signature falsetto warble, segueing into "Silent Night." Couldn't anyone else see that fat scotch pine with the fat frosted lights being swallowed up in a whirlpool of gifts? Open your eyes, people!

But still we waited.

You turned down the rheostat, setting the mood. The Fannie May box of assorted chocolates was passed around in slow motion. Each adult laboring over the description of the chocolates on the box lid, as if it were the last chocolate before lethal injection. As if they were dismantling a bomb. *Do we cut the Raspberry Buttercream wire or the Almond Cluster wire?* Never mind that we just finished three types of pie and Bea's cranberry pudding.

But, finally, Grandma, the Angel of Mercy, from atop the tree—the grandma of "Good Gravy" and even better stuffing—swoops down with her blessing.

An explosion of wrapping paper. A scramble for 9-volt batteries. And, it's done.

You put a stray gift bow on Muffy's head. The dog gets the joke, and she'll play your straight man. And then, you hand out your final gifts. Envelopes. Inside, a savings bond for us grandchildren. Or, a hundred dollar bill. We are in awe. We don't talk about what we've seen in the envelope.

And after the envelopes are passed around, you doze off on the plaid couch.

Eventually, that's where you stayed. Now, almost ninety-three, Grandpa, your glaucoma keeps you anchored to that familiar couch. The tree has gotten smaller—ceramic on the end table—and you have gotten smaller, too.

It has gotten dark. And in your slumber, there is a knock. Here on Christmas Eve. At midnight. Not the trumpeting front doorbell, but a knock at the back door. The porch where good neighbors like Pee Wee Brehm and Doc Fleming were welcomed. You pull yourself to your feet and feel your way around the back of the couch, past the long silent organ.

"Who's there?" you ask.

"It's me, Dad," calls Uncle Kurt. "Open the door."

Confused, you turn the lock, and step out onto that porch. "Hi, Dad. Just got in from Mesa." Uncle Kurt helps you put on your rubber galoshes and houndstooth overcoat. That brown fur hat on your head. And leather gloves. He holds the door open for you, and you step out into the crystalline snow on the deck. Winter air refreshes your lungs. There in the moonlight, is Sam the Siamese cat, with her iridescent eyes, being chased by Muffy who barks, "You better run!" They bound through the snow and into the woods. And you begin to head towards those pines, too, and the glow of the light on the garage. Through the crunch of snow. You fell here a few years ago, but not tonight.

As you tramp through the woods, you see Uncle Mike on his yellow snowmobile, pulling that sleigh with Grandma in her mink coat, bundled under blankets, waving.

"You're a good woman, Benita," you call out, and wave back.

Up ahead on the road, by the garage, Kathy is taking a walk, like every good family should at Christmas. And, back on the deck, Uncle Mark is having a smoke and a good laugh.

You trudge on. Through the pines. Hands in pockets. You round the corner to the garage door. But you are halted in your tracks by the small crowd that has gathered. "Hey buddy, watch where you're going," one of the Magi mutters. Pushing through the sheep, you peer into the garage. Nestled amid the Olds '88, the canoe, and Mike's Kawasaki, is a tired St. Joseph who gives you a wink, and Mother Mary who smiles, beckoning

11

you closer to the Christ Child. But you have no gold, or frankincense, or myrrh. Savings bonds and $100 bills aren't accepted here. All you have is your hat-in-hand. One of the shepherds nudges you forward, "What are you waiting for?" God's good joke is on you. Mercy and grace. Who could have guessed? And, you laugh your good laugh as you bow down before the Christ.

Amen. And, amen.

December 19

This morning it snowed.

Whatever "it" is. The prison gray sky? The weather? God's grace? Yes, grace is the first snow. Today, it's what made you forget that you stopped believing in St. Nick last year. You're even considering listening for talking animals at midnight Christmas Eve.

This morning it snowed.

Tube Socks

"Just some white t-shirts."

My wife had asked what I wanted for Christmas, and then rolled her eyes at my response.

At forty, I can honestly say I would be very happy with a pack of five dependable white t-shirts. Sometimes you can get six for the price of five. Basic. Necessary. Comforting. And what else do I need, honestly?

I have come full circle. When I was a kid, my Grandma White would buy us a pack of tube socks for Christmas every year. We knew exactly what we were going to get, yet she wrapped them every year. Not the most exciting gift, but dependable. Necessary. I can say now that I kind of wished for something else at the time. But what else did I need? Honestly. Here I am decades later, wanting exactly what Grandma White gave us: new underwear. She had discovered the key to happiness and passed that on to us.

And, I remember her gifts. I can't remember what I got last year for Christmas, but I remember that when I was a boy, I got tube socks every year. From Grandma White. In her little walk-up apartment on Clark Street in Stevens Point. With that ornate, wooden German clock, and that picture of my dad in his National Guard uniform. It seemed there was always a Celtics game on. Larry Bird and my grandmother had something going on.

Details.

My dad and stepmom said they weren't going to decorate as much for Christmas this year. "Not as much" would still mean 80% more than the general populace. They transform the entire house at every holiday. I keep telling them it's not necessary on Casimir Pulaski Day. But when they said "not as much" for Christmas this year, my kids protested. "You mean you won't have that Mrs. Claus with the cookie tray? Or the manger scene on top of the TV? Or those cardinals on the mantle? Or…?" My dad said he was surprised at how much they remembered. Kids' memories can be a blessing and a curse. As a result, there will be full-bore decorating this year from my dad and stepmom. My kids cheered.

Details.

I read a quote about faith recently that said it is "…meant to be lived moment by moment. It isn't some broad, general outline—it's a long walk with a real Person. Details count: passing thoughts, small sacrifices, a few encouraging words, little acts of kindness, brief victories over nagging sins."

Details count. That can be said of love, too. It isn't some "broad, general outline." Love is not a parenthesis within a relationship. It's never just implied.

My dad and stepmom love their grandchildren, so they go the extra mile in creating an atmosphere that says "Christmas" to them. My grandma knew my sister hated onions, so she would make her a special dish of potato salad sans onions. My aunts and stepmom steal something from each others' houses each year and wrap it up and give it back to the victim at Christmas. Like a pie server from Thanksgiving, or something. It's a game to see if the others notice what was taken. More details. Noticing. They yowl with laughter on Christmas Eve when they all get together and open their gifts. And my dad told me that he and my uncle get together for coffee every week. Sometimes, my aunt joins them. They take notice of each other. Little things count. I desire that with my brother and sister, too.

Details.

I didn't and don't always get the importance of details. There are regrets. Shortly after I moved to Illinois seventeen years ago and started a new job, my Grandma White died. I drove up and went to the visitation. But I felt like I couldn't stay for the funeral the next day, for some reason. I'm not sure if it was because of obligation, or fear, or just not knowing what my responsibilities were, or just being young and stupid. I should have stayed. I should have taken better notice and immersed myself in the detail of relationship, not just the broad outline.

While she was dying from cancer on my aunt and uncle's couch, I did get to talk to Grandma White one last time. I don't remember exactly what she said, but it had to do with what was most important in her life. Basic. Necessary. Her faith in God. And faith is about details. So is love. Thanks for sharing both of those, Grandma. And for the tube socks.

The Branches Will Fall Down

The Scotch pine sits on the outside, looking in to showcased Frasier firs. Shivering from mange on this thirteen degree night. "How much does this one go for?" I ask.

"Eighteen dollars. The branches will fall down once you get it inside," claims the runny-nosed lot owner. She only looks me in the eye after I pull out my checkbook.

The Scotch pine sits in our living room, making sideways glances. Pretending to look busy, holding up ornaments and lights. Hoping to God, no one exposes him for the imposter he is. It's OK, I'm the one on the other side of the room wearing a Christmas sweater and avoiding eye contact.

The Wisconsin & Illinois Truce of '07

Imagine this. A half-day of school on Friday. Then, the weekend. Then Lincoln's Birthday on Monday. No school. And then, waking up Tuesday to 40 mph winds and 6-12 inches of snow. Snow day! Grace upon grace. My kids' joy spilled over onto the front yard, into tunnels and forts and pirate flags. And, it makes a man want to be charitable.

Except he has to shovel.

I've always thought Illinois winters were rather nancy-pants in comparison to the winters I grew up with in central Wisconsin. The atmospheric conditions of northern Illinois being the armpit of the Midwest. But this January and February, Illinois has been showing her testosterone in the meteorological department. Weeks of sub-zero temps and foot-deep snow that sticks around for weeks. It has felt lately like, well…Wisconsin. Good Lord, I can't believe I'm saying this.

I have spent the better of sixteen years here in northern Illinois defending Wisconsin against the attacks of wounded Bears fans. OK, this is not a difficult outpost to fortify. The enemy's pea shooter volleys usually come against God's country in one of two or three ways:

1. "Those dirty Packers."
2. "Ha. Ha. You said 'bubbler,' 'hotdish,' etc."
3. "Geez-o-Pete, why do you guys label your county roads with letters? Like 'WW'?"

And, when they want to bring out the big guns, I hear: "Cheesehead!" Did I say pea shooter? I meant cap gun.

Anyway, I will not go down like this. Not even to a winter broadside. Donning my union suit, shovel in hand, I trudge out into the battlefield: my driveway.

I like the idea of shoveling. I don't like shoveling, but I like the idea of it. The idea of "real work" with my hands (I don't do much of that in my line of work). And, I like the idea of visually completing a task (I don't do much of that in my line of work, either). So after a few well-aimed thrusts of the shovel blade, I find myself dramatically stretching out my back,

18

now kicking the slush build-up off the mud flaps of the Subaru. And, it's at that point my neighbor—obviously an Illinoisan—comes up with his truck and plow, and says, "Want me to pull the snow out?" My eyes narrow and my pulse quickens. My grip tightens around the shovel. *Play it cool, man,* I remind myself.

"How much are you charging?" I ask.

"Nothing," he says. *What is he trying to pull here?* I wonder. *Keep your hand on your shovel, boy. Let him see you know how to use it.*

"Yeah? Are you sure?"

"Yeah," he says. *Ingenious,* I marvel, *The Trojan Snow Plow.*

"Then I'd love to have you plow us out!" *What the devil am I saying?!?*

And then he did it. He plowed us out.

And, did I mention, another neighbor came with his snow blower and blew out the end of the driveway when we got twelve inches on December 1 of '06? Can you believe it? These are Illinoisans. I am not kidding.

It was on February 13 of '07 that I decided to stop using my shovel for digging foxholes against my friendly Illinois brothers. Instead, I would use it to build bridges. OK, I am kidding about that. I was not going to go that far. But, I had been disarmed, and I would call a truce.

I would begin to see the possibility of good in the people of Illinois.

Of course, there is Abraham Lincoln, the great Commander-in-Chief and emancipator. But, how long can one state play that trump card? OK, they still can, and they should. And besides my Snow Removal Neighbors, there are other good Illinois people in my community. My kids for one. Or, two. They were born in Illinois, which is still hard to admit. But, they are natives, and I like them.

Besides Abraham Lincoln, my Snow Blowing Neighbors, and my kids, there is my son's barber, Chet. There are two beautiful things about Chet. One is that he only gives two types of haircuts: the "Little Boy Haircut,"

19

and then the one he gives to me, which looks remarkably like the "Little Boy Haircut" on my misshapen head. Yet, he wields his combs and clippers with great flair, moving about my son's head like a snake charmer. And, at the end of each haircut, he conjures up a piece of bubble gum, and with sleight of hand, shows the parent for approval before presenting it to the child. The second beautiful thing about Chet the Barber is that he has no hair. I'm enthralled: a man that ministers to the hair needs of others when he cannot grow any of his own. And, he is from Illinois. We saw a sign in his window not long ago: "Chet has retired after forty-eight years." We miss him.

The sixth good person that I have found from Illinois, my friend Wendell, told me something about where we live. Wendell was a history and social studies teacher before he retired. And, he knows everything about gardening, so I tend to believe what he says, despite his state residency. He told me, "You know, Kyle, the Wisconsin state line used to extend just south of where we live." I had that usual eye narrowing and pulse quickening I've experienced from dealing with other Illinoisans. *What is he trying to pull here?* But, I figured, if what he's saying is true about Wisconsin creeping like a glacier, or a receding hairline, into Illinois at one point in history, it explains a lot about Abraham Lincoln, and Chet the Barber, and the three or four other good people I have met so far in the Prairie State. I would then extend my truce to at least February 15. I will keep you abreast of my historical and territorial findings, and of the peace process.

If, on the other hand, he was not telling the truth, truces are easily broken and my trusty shovel is at the ready.

Emmaus Road

"The ice age is coming..." The Clash sang on WAPL as we listened in the dark. We hitched our coats up tighter. Promises falling like snow. Flurries of doubt becoming an avalanche.

The forecast changed that night they both climbed the stairs and gathered us three kids in my room.

"Sorry, but it's over."

I tried to cry hard into my pillow, like I knew I should. Funny how quiet it gets after a snowfall.

From the window in that very room, I used to scan the skies. Up past that white pine to the stars. The Milky Way was a curtain concealing. "Is this all there is?"

And as that glacier began to overtake us, a memory of something my brother said. *"He explained...what was said in all the Scriptures concerning [the Christ]."* As much as I pretended to be sleeping, never wanting to believe that my brother was right about anything, the story struck like flint.

Outside, icicles on the eaves began to drip away. The chattering of teeth giving way to the snap and whistle of kindling. Amen.

GETTING WARMER: Spring

Thaw

We stand on Pebble Beach at Little Sister Bay. Under a brooding March sky. Under a shroud of lamenting gray clouds. We watch the dark waves of Green Bay advance to a rhythmic dirge. We watch them usher down masses of ice that are sick to death of the cold.

"Next please," call the waves to the ice, dashing them on the rocks. Each frozen piece choosing a headstone for winter. Our family stands here at the brink, in the cold wind, watching this ceremony with some reverence. Winter giving way to spring. Even death must die.

We get front row seats. And, a quickening. My wife, our four-year-old daughter, and I throw white rocks into the waves to try to pick off the ice before it ever reaches shore. Gulls circle. We are Israelites pitching rocks at the retreating Philistines, after David has knocked Goliath out stone cold. "Yeah, you better run!" we yell, after a quick look over our shoulders, and one last check for the giant's pulse. "You never had a chance!" we laugh. Our daughter does a victory march, stones clattering in her wake. Our nine-month-old son chants. We are full of life.

A blast of northerly wind shakes our bones and causes us to burrow into our coats. But, it's only a death rattle. Pretty sure.

Yes, winter still lingers. Cold is all around. We don't deny it can even be beautiful and dignified. We just know it's not the end. Pretty sure.

She doesn't know it today, marching on the beach, but five years from now, our daughter will weep in the chapel foyer at her great-grandmother's funeral. One half of the tears will be for her gentle, grace-filled Grandma Bruch, who wore winter so well. The other half of her tears will be for the bitter realization that everyone she knows will die, too, someday. Her mother, her father, her brother, and all the rest. "Why do people have to die?" she will choke out. Maybe more than half of her tears will be allotted for that.

She doesn't know it today, but this girl will be stunned at the audacity of death. Just like every one of us had been at one time. But her faith-filled great-grandma will go quietly to the brink, with confidence that it is not the end. She will go with a God-given white stone tucked in the pocket of her black dress.

Back at Little Sister Bay, our four-year-old skips and gallops, stooping to examine stones along the way. She knows that she has every good reason for a joyful victory march. And, we have every good reason to join her, accompanied by the percussion of ice on the rocks. A gust of wind protests, and we give our coats a hitch out of respect. But back up the road, in the woods, the trillium is signing winter's death certificate. Giants are being felled. Even death is dying.

Harbors & Boat Launches

Tonight's moon is a smooth, bleach-white stone from Pebble Beach at Little Sister Bay. Beckoning to me, all the way down here in Illinois, "Come back! Come back!" It's a strange and wonderful tidal pull. Some kind of anchor I dropped in Door County, Wisconsin, back when I was a little kid. I didn't even know it then. But, it has become a harbor for me.

And harbors, I'm reminded, sometimes do temp work as boat launches.

I think that most of my major decisions have been made in Door County. The decision to move to Illinois after college and begin work with junior high and high school students, had its roots in the rocky soil of Washington Island and the summer youth ministry program of historic Bethel Church. Youth ministry looking, on occasion, like some combination of Jesus and BB gun fights ("Owww! Hey! One pump only!"). Dangerous stuff. And, my wife and I celebrated our honeymoon high on the bluffs of Egg Harbor. Right there on the frightening, exhilarating, beautiful edge. Envisioning our new life together.

More recent decisions have been made in Door County, too. Specifically, most of my recent major decisions have been made in Ephraim. Several years ago, for instance, right there overlooking Eagle Harbor, my wife and I made the choice to resign from a position that I had loved for almost ten years. The decision was excruciating and liberating. Excruciating, because these were people we loved. Liberating, because we asked the questions about our future and the future of our community: "What if...? What could happen?" And, that time in Ephraim set us on a course to pioneer a community development organization focused on at-risk students. I'm not sure it would have happened without the concurrent "lake effect" of harbor and boat launch.

Why is this place such prime real estate for the dual roles of harbor and boat launch? Not too many locations can boast of that kind of holy ground. Certainly, it's the grace of vacation and getting away. It doesn't hurt that generous friends have let our family use their beautiful Ephraim home from time to time, either. Free vacations make me want to be a better man. And I don't mean those "free" vacations, where we've had to listen to "time-share" presentations from someone named Dustin, who, for ninety-plus minutes questioned our values: "Is it just the bottom line with you?

26

This is an investment in your children. You can't put a price on memories, can you?" Vacation time-share presentations do not make me want to be a better man.

But, vacationing in Ephraim has provided the impetus for pushing off the sandbar of routine. For breaking free from the undertow of "That's not how we do things around here," and "Let's be reasonable." Is this true for people who live in Door County, or do they have to go somewhere else to experience this? Maybe Illinois. And, yes, lake breezes and shimmering aspens and lapping waves all help beckon me into harbor and then, later, launch me on towards bigger dreams. But, there is something else, too, about Ephraim. Maybe it's in the name.

Ephraim sounds like the Hebrew word for "fruitful." That's how the Old Testament character came by his name. His father—the great-great-grand-daddy of all dreamers—Joseph, named his second bundle of joy, Ephraim, or "twice fruitful." And, big dreams are what lead A.M. Iverson to take a step of faith across frozen Green Bay in 1853, and envision the fruitful community of Ephraim. So, how can one not be harbored, and then launched, in this atmosphere and rich history of fruitfulness and big dreams? Being in Ephraim makes me think like a dreamer and a pioneer. And, well, like a fisherman. Like the ones dotted all over Green Bay. Can you find bigger dreamers than fishermen? My dream, my fantasy, is to someday catch a fish big enough to eat. It hasn't happened yet. Clinically, there's probably a fine line between dreamers and the insane, but I know it's out there. So, I come to Ephraim—to this heady atmosphere—because I want to be in a place where I can think like a pioneer, and a dreamer, and a fisherman. All of them—us—chasing something we can't see. The deep thing that we know is out there. Now chasing us.

Tomorrow morning, I'll wake here in Illinois, step out on our porch on a cool, clear, breezy spring morning, and my kids will roll their eyes: "I know what Dad's going to say, 'It's a Door County day!'" And it is. Minus the water and trees. Minus the smooth, bleach-white stones. But still, there's some hint on the wind of the grace of Door County. And, of Ephraim. Of harbors and boat launches. The grace of this old man dreaming dreams. Now becoming a young man seeing visions.

Aldo Leopold's Warning

Aldo Leopold, pioneering conservationist and Wisconsin icon, writes in his classic book, *Sand County Almanac*, "There are two spiritual dangers in not owning a farm. One is the danger of supposing breakfast comes from the grocery, and the other that heat comes from the furnace." Farmers or not, we tend to forget the source.

I have a very bad memory. I forget how bad it is.

Not long ago, my wife and I had our annual *Talk*. Maybe semi-annual, I can't remember. *The Talk* occurs when life has become busy and out-of-joint. "It feels like we're living separate lives," she usually says. "Are you okay with this?" And there are tears. And she is right. Our jobs that deal with lots of people, send us off in separate directions. Like we're in two rowboats only catching glimpses of the other as the waves crest, "There! In the distance! Through the mist and spray!" Only to be dropped back into our respective troughs. Stroke by stroke, pulling away.

Our friend says, she recently realized that she's been substituting her "work life" for her "real life." That somehow, home became peripheral. Her family had become a kind of support staff for her "real life"—her faux community of work. We tend to forget the source.

Leopold writes that the cures for these spiritual maladies associated with not owning a farm, are to split a cord of wood, or to plant a garden. I imagine these would cause one to stop, and to consider the source. Probably all of my stunted spiritual growth can be attributed to the deficiency of stopping and considering. Like a skipping rock that flits across the surface of Lake Michigan, only pausing to take what it needs to stay above water. Frictionless living. "And all the fires that crackle here consume but do not burn. All light and no heat…" the dearly departed Mark Heard sang. And, in that kind of consumer atmosphere—whether it be food, or heat, or family, or community, or even God Almighty himself—it all begins to look like it is here to serve me. That it all orbits about my gravity. I need no one. As Leopold observes, that is a great spiritual danger.

That spiritual pioneer and icon, Mother Teresa, wrote, "Sometimes we must ask ourselves questions in order to inform our actions." This is exactly what I don't want: the skip of this stone to be interrupted with a question that would trip me, and drop me below the surface, into the depths.

"Are you okay with this?" my wife asks. There's that sinking feeling. Now gasping for air. It is terrifying. But, maybe drowning is good. Maybe I was just holding my breath anyway, waiting for the inevitable moment my disconnected life would begin to take on water. Maybe you have to go down in order to rise up for your real life.

And, questions, as I said, are usually the things that scrape a hole in the hull of my unanchored life:

Q: Where does this all come from? Not just food and heat, but love and community and breath and wonder and me and…?
Q: How does the way I am living my life right now affect others? From my wife and children, to my neighbor across the street, to my neighbor across the world? By commission or omission? For good or for bad?
Q: What do I need to give? Or, better yet: what do I need to receive? Bishop William Willimon wrote, "I suggest that we are better givers than getters, not because we are generous people, but because we are proud, arrogant people…It's tough to be on the receiving end of love, God's or anyone else's. It requires that we see our lives not as our possessions, but as gifts."
Q: What do I need to stop for God's sake? What do I need to start for my, and everyone else's, sake?

Whether farmers, or not, we tend to forget the source. Are you okay with this?

Indigenous Animals

Trillium. Dandelions. Indian Paintbrush. Milkweed. Daisies. Queen
Anne's Lace. Black-Eyed Susan. Jack-in-the-Pulpit. Purple Coneflower.
Cattails.

The average American can recall 1000 brand names and logos, but can't
name ten indigenous plants or animals. I read that somewhere. I think at a
Starbucks.

Chipmunks. Thirteen-striped ground squirrels. Gray squirrels. Badgers.
Juncos. White-tailed deer. Red-winged blackbirds. Red fox. Prairie
chickens. Yellow perch. Bluegill. Mallards. Sandhill cranes.

I think these flora and fauna are all indigenous to Wisconsin. All off the
top of my head. In fact, I can name two more: black-capped chickadees
and moss. Chickadees were as common as gravel in Amherst, Wisconsin,
where I spent part of my time growing up. And dark green moss was the
carpeting in the white pine woods behind our house. So, don't ask me why,
but in fourth grade I snuck the BB gun out of our garage. My dad didn't
want me playing with it, which is probably why I so wanted—needed—
to do so. So, I snuck the gun out to the backyard and headed off to the
woods, where I spotted a chickadee in one of the pines.

Have you ever seen a black-capped chickadee up close? It's a common
bird, but it is quite striking. Black velvet cap. A black bib. Deep black
eyes. A luxurious gray waist coat, with a downy white breast. And,
an infectious call from which it derives its name: *chik-a-dee-dee-dee*.
Although it has every reason to be aloof and snobbish, it lingers and shows
little apprehension. A gracious innocent among the arrogant, marauding
blue jays and grosbeaks.

Don't ask me why I did it. At first I thought I missed. Dear God, I had
hoped I'd missed. But, never was a truer shot fired. Straight to its mark.
All was quiet. Then, the bird fell over. Still gripping the branch. It swung.
Underneath the branch. For a second. Then. Headlong to the moss below.
A small, black and white form against the emerald floor.

I was horrified. Draped in guilt. Not for fear of getting in trouble for taking
the BB gun out of the garage. That was a misdemeanor.

30

The shock was from killing something beautiful. For as much as a fourth-grader can understand that. Although, maybe fourth-graders have a better eye for beauty than others with 1000 brand names stockpiled in their heads. I was horrified because there was no reason behind what I did. Maybe my first revelation that I had powder and shot packed inside my very own skin.

I didn't set out to shoot a chickadee. Even when I aimed and pulled the trigger, I was thinking I would just see how close I could get. But how does one measure that? Brinksmanship. I didn't mean to shoot the bird. Nor did I mean not to shoot it. Maybe that's the bigger crime. That was the source of my dread.

Afterwards, I stood over the chickadee, gun in hand, with what felt to be a rock on my chest. Years later, one hunter friend told me he would place a berry in the beak of the quail and ring-necked pheasant he would shoot. Maybe even say a prayer. A Native American sign of respect or something. I didn't have enough sense at the time. And the only prayer appropriate would have been one of repentance. All I did was leave the woods and sneak the gun back into the garage. I hid in my room. It wasn't until later, when I couldn't stand myself, that I confessed to my parents. I'm pretty sure I did that.

I can name a few wild things in my backyard today. But, it was in fourth-grade that I began to name the animals and weeds indigenous to my own heart.

Sasquatch

Now I lay me down to sleep. I pray the Lord my soul to keep. And if I die before I wake, I pray the Lord my soul to take. Amen.

This is a prayer we used to say as kids. I didn't remember it until my brother told me he tried it out on his own boys one night recently.

My ten-year-old nephew said he thought it was creepy.

But I didn't remember thinking so back then, when I was six, or seven, or eight, lying under that blue and red plaid comforter. Life was dangerous as a kid, and there was no point in taking chances, even while sleeping. Especially while sleeping. What could possibly be dangerous about being an elementary school kid in central Wisconsin?

Plenty, in the '70s.

I am not talking about the danger that comes from falling out of pine trees, or from being run over by the family station wagon in the dead of winter, or from taking a garbage can cover and a tree branch, climbing onto your bike, and charging at your brother in a joust back there on George Street. I am talking about deeper mysteries that lurk on the edges.

Sasquatch for one. Bigfoot, as he—it—was known to us rural white kids. Only leaving enormous foot prints, tufts of fur, grainy images and trembling children in his wake. That giant ape-like man. What did he want, out there in the woods, watching? I should have been praying for my counterparts in the Himalayas who had it worse: the cold and terrible Yeti. My wife remembers praying to Jesus every night that Bigfoot would stay away. I am glad to report that God answers prayers.

But there were other skulking menaces back then, too, like: Great White sharks, piranhas, killer bees, UFOs, nuclear missiles. At any moment they could've snapped us up. Stripped our flesh. Swarmed us. Abducted us. Fallen out of the sky and laid waste to us. Any one of them. Or all at once. We shivered together as we watched the made-for-TV drama, *The Day After*, and the impending nuclear winter.

All of this, and I have not even mentioned the mysterious danger of liquid nitrogen. Some scientist in a lab coat came to Amherst Elementary School and poured an arctic liquid into a metal container, right there in the gym where we played dodge ball. Then, into that container, he slowly dipped a banana and then dropped it to the tiled floor. *Ta-Daa!* It broke into smithereens like tropical glass. He told us never to touch liquid nitrogen. But what if we came across this inexplicable liquid on the side of the road? That's the information we really needed from that scientist. What if we *accidentally* touched it? What should we do then? Would it creep up our arms like ice from the back of the freezer and turn our flesh solid like petrified banana? Would we break into a million shards? Alone back there on George Street? It could happen.

Although the child's bedtime prayer was mysteriously "creepy," it was an accurate depiction of reality. I was suspicious as a kid, and was pretty sure that life offered no happy endings. In my forties, I am convinced there are no happy endings. Life is a messier, more unpredictable mess than we pretend.

Recently, on Valentine's Day, in the Illinois community where I now live, a grad student opened fire in a university lecture hall. He shot twenty-two people. Six died, including the shooter. I told a friend, who had just gotten his master's from the school, that it was shocking. Right here in our community. He said he wasn't shocked. Sad, but not shocked. He was resigned to the fact that it would happen again.

We talk too much about happiness these days. Scientists in lab coats even study it. My research shows that we should save our breath and our grant money. Happiness is too easily stolen away by Bigfoot, missiles, and shotgun shells. To protect ourselves from cold, lurking devils we must cling to something else that is also below surface. Something more mysterious. Something that extends past the dark woods. We must pray the Lord our soul to keep. Whether we wake or not.

HOT: Summer

Adeste Fideles

"Any big plans for the summer?" I asked.

"Not really. How about you? Let me guess, you're going to Wisconsin?"

"Um, yes."

He smirked, "You know, there are other places besides Wisconsin!"

I smiled on the outside. On the inside, I thought, "Liar."

Here in Illinois, I am surrounded by infidels. No, not faithless, just in denial. Bitter from being left out. By birth, I am a Wisconsinite. I pray for compassion for these Illinoisans as I move amongst them and have my being. However, it does beg the question: Why on earth did I ever move to Illinois in the first place? Missionary work. Father Marquette in reverse. Instead of making new explorations, I invite voyageurs to what Wisconsinites have already discovered: *Adeste Fideles! Come all ye faithful! Taste and see that God's country is good.*

Of course, I say this all in jest, to rib my Illinois brothers and sisters. Or do I? In any case, they're right; I would rather spend time in Wisconsin than anywhere else. At my family's dinner table we ask, "If you could go anywhere on vacation right now, where would you go?" My wife says, "France." My daughter says, "Hawaii." My son says, "Tatooine." And, I say, "Wisconsin." Every time. Obsessive-compulsive? I don't know, am I? I am not alone, though. I have friends whose "Wisconsin" is Texas, or California, or Colorado, or Utah, or Pennsylvania. My lying friend pines for Nebraska. Whatever. Of course, by definition, these places aren't Wisconsin, but they are trying their best.

Why this need for attachments to locations? What makes a person and a place one thing? I'm not sure what it is. Maybe it's like the way people attach themselves to the Packers. If the team pulls off a victory, people say, "WE won!" Or detach themselves after a loss: "Those Packers—THEY played like a bunch of old women!" People connect themselves to winners. But, there's more stability with the "place"—the land—than NFL free agency. So, we connect with the "place"—the land—of Wisconsin for stability. Good memories of beauty and rest are anchored in the granite of this state. We want something more solid than us.

Maybe it's like what Annie Dillard writes of in her short story, "The Living." Her character, Clare Fishburn, observed:

"Here is a solid planet…stocked with mountains and cliffs, where stone banks jut and deeply rooted trees hang on. Among these fixed and enduring features wander the flimsy people. The earth rolls down and the people die; their survivors derive solace from clinging, not to the rocks, not to the cliffs, not to the trees, but to each other. It was singular. Loose people clung in families, holding on for dear life. Grasping at straws! One would think people would beg to be tied to trees."

The Wisconsin River—the hardest working river in the world, we were always told—is "fixed and enduring." It is still there. The very one that I swam in as a boy during family reunions and birthday parties for my Great-Grandma Diver. There are no more reunions, but the river is still there. Even the beautiful and kind Grandma Diver, who lived to 101: she crossed the Jordan River into Beulah Land. She's gone, but the Wisconsin River is still there.

So, in the busyness and relentless rush of time, I grab a hold of the solid rocks of Door County and the great pines of Nicolet. I rest in the steady waters of Lake Michigan and the Wolf River. But, no, that's not quite it. It's more than a solitary clinging to the land. Fishburn was wrong. It is also, obviously, people. My connection to the place—Wisconsin—is invariably linked to the people. Person and place become one thing with the glue of others. Community.

Amelia Diver understood this.

When our family would pick her up in our yellow station wagon, from her yellow cracker box house, in her yellow coat, and drive from Stevens Point to Wisconsin Rapids, along the wooded Wisconsin River, she would squeeze in the backseat with us three kids. Wedged in, we would always ask, "Do you have enough room, Grandma?" Her reply was always, "If I have this much room in heaven I'll be happy." Those humble words gave me, as a boy, a picture of community and of heaven. This attachment is a desire for place, yes, and for people. And, something—someone— permanent.

Sweet Corn

This is the summer of plowing the crops under. A time of drought and brush fires. It's the year of dead limbs and diseased trees. A season of grass that rarely sees the mower.

But today, on the west edge of town, down by the grain elevator: sweet corn. A blue pick-up from out of town piled high with fat green and flaxen ears. Some storehouse of hope two counties over.

And at my grandma's cottage on Lake Sherwood in July, we used to eat that corn-on-the-cob and pretend we were typewriters. Tap. Tap. Tap. Ding. Return. Slide. Journalists with salt and butter hands reporting that the forecast calls for rain.

Circus World Museum

The small town of Baraboo, Wisconsin, is home to the Circus World Museum. Fifty-acres of circus history in the town that the Ringling Brothers used as their winter quarters from 1884 to 1918. I remember my grandparents taking us there when we were little. Actually, my grandma would take us. My grandpa was simply the chauffeur. Hair slicked back, wrapped in a gray cardigan, and holed up in his air-conditioned Oldsmobile, my grandpa would hide behind his newspaper, monitor the Brewers game, and wait for us to come out. All the while, Mother Mary shivered on the dashboard. And, as we walked in, there was a fake, yet terrifying, gorilla in a circus train cage. But, what if he suddenly wasn't, well, fake? It could happen. Next to him was a trumpeting, wheezing calliope. (One time, I remember a reporter on Channel 5 doing a feature on the calliopes of Circus World Museum. He pronounced it "CA-lee-ope," like it rhymed with antelope, through the entire, well-researched segment.) The monster ape and a gasping cacophony welcomed us into the museum. I remember being afraid of what I would see.

Not long ago, in July, my family and I visited this historical site on the way to go camping at Devil's Lake. Twenty-five years after my last visit, probably. And it is beautiful. My kids loved it. In one building, at the Circus World Museum, there are cracked black-and-white photos of faithful elephants. In another display, there is a scratchy, hollow recording of a ringmaster calling the Big Top into glorious action. And, over there, in a glass case, are faded garments covered in dull sequins, once worn by the Flying Wallendas and other high-wire risk takers. Next to them, a case full of clown props used to show up human absurdity.

Just up the hill from there, are housed dozens upon dozens of ornate, shiny circus wagons, once used to carry this show to cities around the nation. And, then, there is this red and white sideshow tent outside, where there are wax mannequins of giants, snake handlers, a tattooed woman whose skin looks like a map and tells some mysterious story, and Siamese twins who are connected one to another with a bond I could never understand.

Twice a day, there is a Big Top show on the hot, dusty grounds, with some very tired looking clowns, and a sleepy organ player, where the most active member of the event is the attendant with the shovel who runs along behind the elephants.

All that to say, I'm not sure there should be a circus museum. It's all very interesting and beautiful, but where is the thunder? Where is the clatter of hooves and wheels taking this show on the road? Where is the glory of this strange spectacle, the likes of which the world has never seen? Is this where children are supposed to run away to? See, I'm not so sure there should be a museum for circuses. Why? Because the very essence of the circus is movement. Don't fence it in and flatten it out. It's about bringing risk, danger, excitement, wildness right to peoples' front doors. So, to reduce it to permanent displays, models, and reminiscence that requires us to come to it is, at best, looking through the wrong end of the telescope. At worst, it is a denial of the circus' reality. No offense intended towards the Wisconsin State Historical Society, but I suggest they free those elephants from the leg shackles of "used-to-be" and "remember-when." We need them now more than ever.

Maybe that's why my grandpa wouldn't come in, but sat in the car with Mother Mary and Paul Molitor. Maybe he was afraid of what he wouldn't see.

Of course, I am not talking about the Circus World Museum.

Hey There

"Hey there," I call out to others while walking this afternoon on County G in Egg Harbor, Wisconsin. It curves around cedar and birch and rocky bluffs. It's a good, blue-sky, lake-breeze day to greet people. I don't know how "hey there" became my signature greeting, as opposed to, say, "hi," "howdy," "hello," etc. Or, "Yellow!" as we so hilariously answered the phone as kids.

By "hey there," I guess I mean that you are over there, and that by the process of elimination, I am over here. It's the extent of my knowledge of physics. By speaking my "hey there," I like to think I am somehow spanning the distance between us. I infuse it with as much warmth and respect as I can. Elderly folks seem to appreciate it the most. Adolescents are usually in shock. But, I think my "hey there" will bridge the gap. Maybe even change the world. Maybe. Some people nod or smile. Others say hello. And, still others ignore me and say nothing. The last group I always assume is on vacation from Chicago.

Residents of Washington Island, Wisconsin have it figured out. Washington Island—despite being only six by five miles—has one of the oldest and largest Icelandic settlements in America. I confess that my mental picture of Icelandic people is tattered and faded; it doesn't allow them the display of warmth or hospitality. I think of grave, black-and-white fishing boat captains and their severe, black-and-white wives, somber and cold as cod. No offense, Iceland. It's me, not you. It probably comes from watching too much television and consuming too many frozen fish sticks as a child.

Anyway, this Icelandic crowd surprised me. Every driver, it seems, on Washington Island has his or her own wave. Not really a traditional wave—as hands never leave the steering wheel—but subtle variations of finger movements that make each driver's gesture his own.

There is the slow index finger arc from left to right, reminding the oncoming driver of the path of the sun in the sky. A metaphor for the passage of time and the importance of tending to friendships in the time we're given.

Actually, I just made that up. I have no idea.

But, whether it's the quick, confident index finger salute, like a mailbox flag, or a twirling, gunslinger gesture ending in a *pistola* aim-and-shoot, the motivation is the same: *Hey there*. Bridging the gap. I only lived on the island for two summers, and yet I received the same neighborly treatment as someone who'd lived there for sixty years. I spoke to one islander, who was born and raised there, and she told me that she had never, in fact, left the island in *her* sixty years. Not even so much as a ferry trip to the mainland. I was in disbelief when she told me, and all I could think was, "Poor castaway." But, now, as I consider these common friendly gestures (hey, I know they're not monumental, but they could be a lot worse), maybe I understand why she never felt the need to leave.

Yes, people grouse about the sham humility of Midwesterners and the faux graciousness. But, maybe there is something to be said for polite acknowledgement. A warm regard. That initial gesture of neighborliness. Because it is rare. Sam Smith, writer and activist, observes, "I feel the vacuum, the loneliness, the dehydration of the soul as people...still wander the streets without knowing how to say *hi* to one another." Take a visual survey—walk downtown or in your local Big-Mart—there is a veneer of defensiveness and suspicion surrounding human interaction today.

Maybe neighborliness is one of those things you learn from the outside in. A waving hand, or friendly gesture sets the rest of the body and soul on a path towards being a neighbor. Polite regard may even help us do what's right. I've heard that pre-WWII the British people had the same animosity towards Jews as the Germans had, yet British manners wouldn't allow for the same kind of persecution.

A wave or a "hey there" puts us in a position to know the other person. To bridge the gap. And, from there, who knows, maybe our neighbors' concerns might even become our own concerns. It's a small thing, I know, but if you are ever on the receiving end of my "hey there," would you at least pretend to acknowledge me over here?

Then we can go from, well, there.

Job's Wisconsin

The book of Job, chapters 38-41; a paraphrase:

Tell me, who is it that churns up the mighty Wolf River like a cheap washing machine for you at Big Smokey Falls?

Have you ever rounded up herds of mosquitoes and sent them on their summer stampede?

Do you know why the ferocious, but slow, snapping turtle springs his jaws like a trap and won't let go?

Who can call up Aurora Borealis for a command performance above Nicolet, as you lie on your back in the long wet grass? She dances through several wardrobe changes, and there you sit slack-jawed and prostrate.

Can you pour humidity through a sieve upon old women and play havoc with their permanents? Or send forth the sun's heat so fierce that white central Wisconsin thighs stick to black vinyl car seats?

Can you pull in a trout with a fishhook or put him in a net? Or, are you only privy to where the bluegill lives? Have you ever caught a fish big enough to eat, or fried one in a pan, under the moon at Devil's Lake?

Do you know why all the traffic gets dammed up on I-90, just south of Madison, precisely when your bladder is about to rupture? Tell me if you do. And then begins to flow again as if nothing happened?

And who endowed the bald eagle with eyes that can see for a mile? Even around that bend in the Wolf River, to see if we're still together.

Firework

My mother called me. Then, my brother called and said, "It's his independence day." Grandpa Halverson passed away on July 4th in Port Edwards, Wisconsin. He was ninety-four. I'd meant to call him that week.

I was at a fireworks display with friends when I got the news. Grandpa was worth crying over right then and there. And, soon the fireworks started. Whistles and green rockets bursting into pinwheels. Thunder and white blooms crackling and plummeting to earth. Booms and red corkscrews in whirling dervish. An overwhelming display.

In between all of that—in those split seconds of darkness—are the ghosts. Those almost undetectable columns and wisps of gray-white smoke against black sky. One for each firework. They float off with the wind, exiting stage left. A slow drift parade. A flickering silent film.

And then onto the next flash and bang.

Underneath all of this, in the band shell, is the city municipal band conjuring up a frenzied set of show tunes, marches, and patriotic numbers. Unable to see any of the display going on right above their heads. They miss it all. Year after year.

Life is too much. Too fast. I miss a great deal of it.

Someday, I intend to run for city council on the platform that we change the annual *fireworks* display to the annual *firework* display. After we all take our seats on blankets and lawn chairs, there will be one firework. We can marvel at its light, and its color, and its sound, and its smell, and its shape against the darkness. And, its pall as it passes.

Then we will move our mouths in awe and shake our heads in astonishment: *Will you look at that? Good Lord, can you believe it?* And, we won't help but wonder about such beauty. *How was it made? Who can take it all in?*

Then we will go home trembling in silence. It will be worth crying over right then and there.

GETTING COLDER: Autumn

To Whom It May Concern

To Whom It May Concern,

I am writing to recommend Autumn for the position recently left vacant by Summer. I have observed Autumn's work for the last forty years or so, and feel I am as qualified as anyone to comment on her abilities.

For at least the past forty years, Autumn has faithfully, and without complaint, ushered in Packer football seasons, kicked-off school years, and provided meaningful work for sweater manufacturers and kids with rakes. She has been a major sponsor of the annual harvest of pumpkins, apples, cauliflower, brussels sprouts, and zucchini, to name a few. I don't even have to mention how each year she hosts that beloved children's event: Halloween. And, of course, her crowning achievement: the fall color display in collaboration with the trees of our community. Her management skills have allowed all of these to come off like clockwork. Of course, it would be difficult in this space to elaborate on all of her accomplishments.

I understand that in the eyes of a few, Summer has left some big shoes to fill. However, sometimes big shoes just mean they were on the clearance rack. As you consider Autumn for this position, let me be candid: this has not been a stellar year for Summer. Yes, there was that sunny week in June, and the fireworks were OK, and the spinach came up nicely. But, personally, I think any loudmouth with an associate's degree in P.E. could do what Summer does. This year, I am sure many would agree, she phoned it in. Like the waiter at that lakeside bar and grill, who seemed so friendly and funny at first: "How's it goin', Boss? What can I do you for?" Ha. Ha. Ha. But he was nowhere to be found when it came to refilling your Diet RC Cola, or bringing that bottle of A.1. Steak Sauce after you'd asked for it three times. If he thought he was going to escape without eating one of my signature piercing glares in tip reduction sauce, he was deluded. Anyway, if you check the time cards, Summer showed up late for the first day of work. About three weeks late, as I recall. And there were days, even weeks on end, where she was absent without as much as a phone call. For example, my one week of vacation: sixty-three degrees and rainy. Come on! This is July 30, people! Any chimp with *The Old Farmer's Almanac* could have done a better job.

But enough about Summer's lack of aptitude, I am writing on behalf of Autumn. I understand this is just seasonal work, but Autumn's abilities cannot be overstated, and she would be perfect to pick up where Summer left off. In fact, she would bring a necessary change of direction. After the mindless, devil-may-care stupor that Summer left us with, you will find that Autumn will create a much-needed atmosphere of introspection: *How did we do this year? What will we do with the time we have left? Who can we give all this zucchini to?*

I highly recommend Autumn to you for this opportunity. She is clearly the next logical step for your organization. Thank you for your consideration. Kind Regards.

Hunting for Words

As soon as I walked in, I knew something was wrong. Blood was spattered at the entry way and then up each step. Large drops. More blood on the landing. Up the second flight. Through the second floor fire door.

And, the trail stopped. At room 201. I knocked nervously.

"Come in."

And, there he was. A bloody knife in his hand.

"What did you do, Rick?" I asked in disbelief. But, it was obvious; his victim lay in plain view. Limp. Lifeless. Who would've imagined, here in Stevens Point, Wisconsin? Right here in my college dorm. Actually, it wasn't too hard to believe. Rick was also the one who would hang upside down in his closet from gravity boots. And, wear shorts, when it was twenty below, on the way to class. It was only a matter of time.

"Why? How?" I stammered.

"It was easy," he explained, "I just opened the window and took my shot. Never saw it coming."

"A shot with what?"

"My blowgun," he said.

"What? You have a blowgun?"

"Yeh."

"You shot all the way from the second floor?"

"Yep," he said proudly.

"Nice shot," I exclaimed.

"Thanks. Yeah, I saw the rabbit in the bushes and nailed it with a dart."

And, Rick proceeded to skin that rabbit at his study desk. Right there in front of us in his dorm room. This was central Wisconsin. No big deal. He grew up hunting, like everyone else.

Well, except me.

I've never been hunting. Which is probably fine. I like the idyllic picture of it. Like I like fishing. The solitude and the search. But, my fear would be that I would actually shoot something. Or catch something: "Dear God, now what?"

Often, I think, writing is like hunting. Or at least chasing rabbits in a thicket. I know some people say that the writing is "in them." They just have to dig it up. I'm not that confident in myself as a rich container. I actually think that words are "out there." They are elusive and wild. It feels, for me, that they have to be chased. Hunted. Baited. Coaxed. Called. Tracked.

Thus, I am in adulation when a word actually wanders into my sights. In deep thanksgiving when I can dress one on my desk. In awe when I can put a few together on my stringer. Lord, I am a dork: "Ah-yep. Just got back from a word hunt. Look at the size of this 900-word beauty. Had to land her with MS Word '98, but it made for a good fight. O' course I'm gonna have her mounted." My Uncle Mike would be none too impressed; he gets 300-point bucks and 300-pound muskies every season.

But, in writing, as in hunting, you have to strike while the iron is hot. And, in order to strike the hot iron, or whatever, you have to, well, check the temperature of the iron regularly, or however it works. You gotta show up. Like Rick from his second floor window. He was ready to strike. Eyes peeled and blowgun at the ready. Or, the guy in his underwear, you always hear about, who shoots the buck from his kitchen window while he's drinking his coffee. Why does that guy keep his rifle right there next to the creamer? That was probably Rick, too. But, last week, I jumped out of the shower 'cause I had to write something down for fear of losing it. I ended up forgetting to wash my hair. I probably wouldn't have to do that if I just showed up each day and wrote. I would catch more rabbits that way.

Often, however, I don't have the wherewithal for the chase. Actually, I am forcing myself to stay in this "word blind" right this very minute. Well, it's not really a duck blind or a tree stand. It's a chair at the Drink Coffee café in Sister Bay. But, I could bolt at any second, and check my e-mail. Or go to the bathroom. Or buy another coffee. Or check my e-mail. Maybe I'm afraid of what I'll catch if I write too much. Or, the work of hauling it in. So, I am envious of all my prolific writer friends who can churn out words daily. They are more brave than I. It's said that the famous and prolific Wisconsin writer, August Derleth, could crank out 5000 words a day—15,000 if he needed to. Courageous jerk.

Less a hunter, I am more like a driver hoping to hit a deer. Serendipitous, glorious road kill; the prey, the capture, the gutting, the vehicle for delivery, all at the same place at the same time. Do you remember that story a few years ago, of the dozen or so white tails in Wisconsin that got on a highway overpass and ended up jumping over the guard rail? Head over hoof. Deer raining from above onto the interstate and cars below. If only I were that lucky.

The Muse

I am trying so hard here. Sitting down in hard chairs in quiet places. Trying to look the part and do what I think they do. Away from all the distraction. Awaiting The Muse. I'm not sure who she is or what she looks like. Maybe it's the girl at the next table who breathes from her mouth and bounces her leg. Who tries to hide hay fever snorting. Now drumming her fingers. Maybe she has a secret to whisper into my ear: "Special delivery of words for you, Mr. White. Please sign here." There should be a uniform and schedule, like for tooth fairies and UPS guys.

Raising Ebenezers

I have a confession to make. When I've visited Door County, Wisconsin, I've taken a few things. Not stealing really. But not really borrowing. I confess that I've taken some of the smooth, white stones unique to the beaches there. Now, I think that it's illegal to remove rocks from Washington Island. I've never done that. Honest. When I lived on Washington Island, in the employ of historic Bethel Church's summer youth ministry program, I do remember enjoying fires on the beach with friends, and then suddenly, one of the cold rocks would explode from the heat. We all would scramble from the stinging shrapnel. The place left its mark. And, I remember making painful, barefoot pilgrimages across rocky beaches only to be baptized in the frigid waters of Lake Michigan. So, no, the rocks were not my friends on Washington Island. I never pocketed any of them.

Later, however, as I began to more deeply appreciate Door County as a place of rest and reorientation, I started to see the smooth rocks as relics. Sacred mementos. Now, the "Sacred Memento" defense probably wouldn't hold up in court, but let me build my case. It all started innocently, where our family would take some watercolors (non-toxic), sit on the dock, and paint a few rocks. Pictures of sunsets, the place where we were staying, sailboats, and seagulls. Or, in the case of my two-year-old, at the time, greenish-brown rainbows. An innocent pastime. You understand, don't you?

But, it is true that we began to take a few rocks home, and that they have begun to accumulate in a copper bowl on our coffee table. And, it's become more than just paint on the rocks. We've begun to write on them, too. On the flipside of tempera painted lighthouses you can read, in tiny print, about our adventures at Nicolet Bay Beach and the Door County Maritime Museum. We've chronicled our time at Wilson's Restaurant & Ice Cream Parlor, Pebble Beach, and Peninsula State Park sunsets. And, monumental events, like my wife's encounter with the "best roast beef sandwich ever" at the deli in Sister Bay, and my son's trip to the Sturgeon Bay emergency room after swallowing a quarter.

It's even become our end-of-summer ritual to go out to dinner as a family and record on one of the rocks all the memorable events that took place. And, no longer just rocks from Door County. We lift rocks and other relics from other corners of the world, too. Stone diaries of momentous events. Pivotal times of decision. If you sorted through them, you'd see: a Chicago rock from 2003 that lists my wife's first triathlon at age thirty-five and (not to be outdone) my daughter's first kids' triathlon; a piece of jagged granite that marks a camping trip with friends at Devil's Lake, where it rained for thirty-six hours straight; a pine knot from Mexico, where we spent part of a summer building houses with a cool group of high school students; a piece of sandstone that simply states "Step o' Faith May 2K" from when I resigned from a job to pursue the next step in our lives; a seashell from June 2001—I can't remember what that's from; and, a rock with my daughter's crude drawing of planes crashing into a building from September 11, 2001.

These relics have become a chronicle of our life together. Reminders. Truth be told, the rocks are exercises in thanksgiving. Is "thanksgiving" a good defense? 'Cause, there's a long history of rocks in relation to thanksgiving. Remember the old church hymn, "O Thou Fount of Every Blessing?" If you do, you'll remember snickering at the second verse, because it starts with, "Here I raise my Ebenezer, Hither by Thy help I've come…" And, after snickering, you'll remember having thought, "What the devil is an Ebenezer?" Well, our Bible reading today, brethren, is from the Old Testament in 1 Samuel, chapter 7 and verse 12. After the Israelites drop-kicked the Philistines, the prophet Samuel erected a great rock monument and named it "Ebenezer" or, translated from Hebrew, 'stone of help.' And, whenever the Israelites saw the stone memorial, they would remember that God had helped them. They would remember divine grace and mercy. But, not surprisingly, the exact site of the Ebenezer is no longer known. Which may stand as a memorial to our languishing attention spans. We need lots of reminders when it comes to thanksgiving. Hence, the entire bowl of rocks in our house.

As I began to write this, my six-year-old son brought in a handful of gravel from the side of the road in front our house, and laid it on the kitchen table. "Look at these, Dad!" Some red granite, some quartz and some other spotted stones. To him, they were treasures. In fact, everything is treasure to him. Everything is amazing. Blue jay feathers, tree bark, bottle caps, a crayfish claw, a flattened Matchbox car from the alley. He has boxes and pockets full of Ebenezers and knows the exact site of each one. As writer and musician Terry Scott Taylor sings about the miraculous found in the mundane, "No, nothing really happened….There was laughing and crying / The sky was blue / And the grass was green…. The sea reached the shore….The moon came up / When the sun went down….It was an ordinary / Extraordinary day / It was a very ordinary / Extraordinary day / In every way."

So, I confess. I'm guilty. But, perhaps, if I'm guilty in regard to pilfering stones, relics, and Ebenezers, it is because I haven't pocketed enough of them. They are everywhere. In the smooth, white stones of Door County and in the very gravel around my house.

Reading Room

I read that one edition of the *Wall Street Journal* has more information than one of the Pilgrims would've ingested in a lifetime. I'm not sure who figured that out, but I do know that my brother spent thirty minutes in the bathroom, after Thanksgiving turkey and stuffing at my mom's, reading the *Stevens Point Journal*. He doesn't live in Stevens Point.

Much of my reading is done on the toilet these days. Out with the old, in with the new. Like some bulimic librarian: Binge. Purge. Binge. Purge. The constant rolling flow of this microfiche brain.

If I were ever to be alone with myself in my head, I'd probably pick up a magazine and pretend to read.

Coming Late

I come to things late in life.

Like coffee. And chess. And beer.

Coffee because, like many things, I liked the idea of it, but not the taste. Until one night, a few years ago, I had a writing deadline and drank eight cups. Wow, man. I went from McDonald's coffee to Americanos in a matter of hours. I have not looked back.

Regarding chess, I don't take directions well. Directions for games, or driving, or assembling things. I figure someone else will listen for me. But recently, I sat still long enough for a junior high kid to teach me. I think it is amazing. Whoever thought of chess, had a great idea.

Beer is more involved. I grew up United Methodist, and alcohol was not looked upon kindly, thus it didn't figure into my faith line-up. And I've become aware of how big alcohol companies target advertising in poor communities. But starting in my thirties, I started to enjoy a beer once in awhile with friends. Is sticking with smaller breweries more ethical? Is Leinenkugel's a small brewery? I am not in danger of becoming drunk, however, as I get sleepy after one beer. I wouldn't be able to stay up long enough to become an alcoholic. Benjamin Franklin, a fine statesman and inventor, but not-so-hot theologian, tried this route: "Beer is living proof that God loves us and wants us to be happy." Um. OK. Maybe.

I'm sad that I missed out on these "social lubricants." I mean "social lubricant" in the best of ways. A vehicle to sit and talk. I read an essay by a woman who wished that she smoked cigarettes. She longed for the "do nothing," no-excuse-needed, sit-and-chat opportunity that the "smoke break" afforded her fellow employees.

I come to things late in life. I've also come late to coming-to-terms. Introspection. But I'm starting now that I'm in my forties. Some evidence of that is, uh, crying at movies. It's only been a few. Really. Two or three. Four, tops. It started with the film *Big Fish*. Especially, the scene at the end where the father's larger-than-life life is coming to an end, and his son carries him to the river. I could hardly see the road driving home from the theatre that evening. My wife was good about not laughing at me. And, it wasn't a fluke. Every time I've watched it since, I can't hold back. Other films, too, like *Finding Neverland, Second-Hand Lions, Forrest Gump,* the 1950s version of *Cheaper By The Dozen*, life insurance commercials, etc. You may think I am a nancy-pants, or overly-sensitive. I swear that I am not. But someone said that if you find yourself choked up, or in tears, you should camp there for awhile, as it's probably the signal of a spiritual break in the dam. The writer of one of the wisdom books in the Old Testament, Ecclesiastes, said, "The heart of the wise is in the house of mourning; but the heart of fools is in the house of mirth."

The common thread throughout these? Fathers and sons. Loss. Not a place I want to camp. But the truth is, I miss my dad. You'd think he was dead by what I said, but he is not. He will not eat most fruits or vegetables, but he is alive and well, enjoying retirement. Golfing. Trying to thwart the squirrels at the birdfeeders. So more accurately, I missed my father. By that, I mean I missed out on close proximity fathering because my parents divorced when I was in middle school.

This is not an indictment, or way to garner pity. It's just reality. It—this thing that is missing, or that I missed—didn't register until I was in my thirties, after I became the father of a son.

(Last weekend, I went to a funeral visitation with my middle school daughter. Her friend's dad died at the age of forty-two. So, this boy and his mom had to stand next to the casket for five hours while people filed through, trying to offer some word of comfort. And, the boy, in a jacket and tie, kept saying, "Thank you for coming," while fighting back tears and shifting his weight from one foot to the other. My daughter and I just hugged and cried a little bit after we got through the line. "It's a sad, lonely, rotten world….it's a sad, lonely, rotten, damn world," musician David Wolfenberger sings. That is one of the truest songs I've ever heard. It's true for sons, and it's true for dads.)

In my line of work, I am around a lot of middle school guys whose fathers are out of the picture. These boys don't do very well. The statistics are ridiculous. Luckily, my dad was close by, and tried, and took us places and all that. I love him. But still, I think, with divorce, there are things that are missed, or forfeited. I have always wanted more with my dad. He is going to be sixty-seven this year. As I turned forty, I wanted to make it a priority to get to know my dad better. I don't want to say, "Well, it is what it is."

One Wisconsin value is: "Do the best with what you have." Usually, that's a good reminder to persevere and be creative. Like using bread bags as liners in winter boots. Or like the "mock chicken legs" we had for dinner growing up. No one's heard of them in Illinois. But these grease fried, ground veal and pork creations, molded around wooden skewers to look like chicken drumsticks, were the product of a time when chicken was expensive. A little more time spent on naming them would have been worth it, but they were pretty good. Someone did the best with what they had.

Sometimes, though, "Do the best with what you have," is the very opposite of perseverance and creativity. It is the white flag of settling. A dull and slothful response to life. Worse, a complete lack of faith. As if this is the best we can do, while we live Thoreau's life of "quiet desperation." I don't want to settle. But maybe even the desperation is evidence of something more. That's good news for me. I have a longing for more with my father because I believe there is an innate sense of God as Father. That opens up at least a few possibilities. I've come to this realization late, but I don't want to miss the opportunity.

Someone told me a few years ago, that one doesn't really become a man until his father dies. I have no idea what that means, but I hope that it's not the case—his death any time soon, or the idea that my maturity hinges on that event. I think next time I visit him in Wisconsin, I will see if he wants to go have coffee. Or a beer.

Mock Chicken Legs

Ingredients:
- ½ lb veal, ground
- ½ lb pork, ground
- ½ lb beef, ground
- ¾ tsp salt
- ½ tsp pepper
- Poultry seasoning, to taste

Additional:
- 1 egg, beaten
- Bread crumbs
- Butter
- Meat skewers

Directions:
Blend all of the ingredients. Press mixture on skewer in shape of chicken leg. Roll in beaten egg and bread crumbs and fry in butter until golden brown. Place in oven at 350°, add drippings from pan and bake 35 minutes. Makes about 8.

Postcards from the Edge of the Bluff

"I didn't have the same sense of place as you did growing up," my friend told me. He grew up in Iowa.

I told him, "I don't think I did either."

Did anyone? Growing up in Wisconsin, I was as unimpressed as anyone is of his home. The same Thrifty-Mart. The same Richard's Drive-In. The same ratty city Christmas decorations. The same neighbors. The same patch of grass to be mowed. Week after week. God, who could stand it another day?

But, something changed upon moving away from Wisconsin. I began to miss something. I realized that much of my identity was rooted in Wisconsin. Certainly, that's been accentuated by my friends in Illinois. Part of our poking and jabbing is based on the "enmity" between the two states. The Packers vs. Bears rivalry is a big part of that. And the whole "cheesehead" thing. The old joke: Q) What's the difference between a Cheesehead and a Butthead? A) The Illinois state line. Except Wisconsinites don't say "butt."

Right now I am closing in on my fortieth birthday. Part of my wife's gift to me was a weekend of camping at Devil's Lake. By myself. My favorite camping spot. I asked for it, but am realizing as I type this that, hey, it may have been a gift for her. And friends who I told about this getaway said, "That's weird," and "You're kidding…by yourself?" Is it really that weird, and am I really that bad of company? But the gift for me is to get back here to Wisconsin to write. Such fertile ground. What a glorious gift.

It's smooth sailing up I-90 to Baraboo. The entrance to Devil's Lake is a tunnel to another world. Dense woods only allow for a few shafts of sunlight. The drive curves around rock walls and bluffs, until the lake expanse opens up at the bottom. My anticipation is high.

The tent goes up easily, and the Ice Age camping loop is empty. It's October. A postcard picture of what I was hoping for. I pull out the laptop, pull up a chair, and prop my feet on the picnic table. *Sigh*. Flipping through my index card book of ideas, I am aware of the quiet and of the leisurely descent of yellow leaves. Isn't this the kind of time and place that

62

writers dream of?

That Friday afternoon, I start or finish three different essays. Very productive for me. Writing is usually a chore.

I celebrate with a fish fry. There are no good fish fries in Illinois, unless rubber is a kind of fish. One of the park rangers recommends the Baraboo Country Club. It's pretty good. All-you-can-eat, with a Leinie's Creamy Dark. My table overlooks the rolling golf course and gives a view straight between the two bluffs at Devil's Lake. Isn't this the perfect weekend? I'm obviously out-of-place with my camping clothes. Some country club people talk loudly at the table next to me. I try to jot down some notes on a writing assignment I brought along. Why did I bring it along at all? So people wouldn't think it was weird that I was eating by myself?

Or maybe I'm not too good with solitude.

I'm reminded of this back at camp, as I sit in my tent alone. It's October and it gets dark by six or seven o'clock. I go for a walk. I start a fire and try to be introspective. Fifteen minutes later, I give in and watch an episode of *Deadwood* on my laptop. I'm in fitful sleep by nine. So much for the idyllic writer's retreat.

I came here to write. I did that. The question, however, this weekend is: *Why write at all?* There is writing that informs and instructs, of course, but I think most writing—songs, novels, essays, and probably "inform and instruct" writing, too—has the same motivation at its core. That motive is summed up in the simplest writing form. Not the poem or the haiku, but the postcard. Our family keeps a small wooden box of the postcards we've received. They range from Paris to Wisconsin Dells. From Mongolia to Rib Mountain State Park. From Turkey to Ehlenbach's Cheese Chalet in DeForest. But all of their messages can be summed up in the classic sentiment: "I love you. Wish you were here." I like you. Don't forget me.

Why write? To love and to be loved. I write because "I wish you were here." The "here" being inside my head. A scary thought? But my writing self is probably my truest self. I write to know and to be known. I write to send a postcard.

Ironically, I went away by myself for the weekend to write. I isolated myself in order to "know and to be known." What the heck? If I have a sense of "place" here in Wisconsin, it is because of the people I have experienced it with. If Devil's Lake is one of my favorite places to be, it is because of the people I have shared it with and continue to share it with.

Saturday morning, I am up at 6 a.m. The tent is down by 7:30. I write a bit more, but I leave Devil's Lake for home by noon. I had the opportunity to stay quite a bit longer. And yes, there is a time for solitude. But this weekend, I'd rather be with those people who know me and whom I know.

We will make plans to return to Devil's Lake next summer. Together.

Mountain Biking is Grace

It's a cool September morning in Wisconsin. I'm writing this in my head as I motor up a hill at Kettle Moraine State Park. Sunlight percolates through pines and poplars. Grunting, almost asthmatically, I make the crest of the hill as sweat slips out from under my bike helmet. I thank God for the steep decline that opens up before me. The blessing for my work. The fruit of my toil.

I launch my mountain bike down the 55-degree-angled slope that's wet from rains the day before and muse: "This is the intro for my article! Right here, baby!" The rush of air buzzes across my helmet straps. My legs and arms stiffen as I rumble down the gully-ripped, rock-studded trail—rocks, in fact, the size of grapefruits and cantaloupe. "Baby heads," in mountain bike lingo.

I squeeze the brakes to avoid a rut. The tire grabs, while the rear end slides on the moist dirt, then vaults. I am airborne, wondering where this fits into my essay. And, in Super Slo-Mo, I arc through the ether. Now descending, my helmet crunches on one of the cantaloupe rocks. Second point of contact: right shoulder with rocks and gravel. Third: right forearm between my body and trail. Did something "pop?" Fourth, fifth, sixth, seventh, eighth: various limbs, parts, and digits co-mingle with assorted rocks, sand, and bike parts, including, but not limited to, an unnatural coupling of a brake handle with my inner thigh. I'm spread like chain grease on the rocks.

A pregnant pause.

The dust settles, and I check for missing parts. A hole in my shirt. Some blood, some abrasions, some imbedded gravel, and some tender spots that will give birth to bruises tomorrow. But nothing broken or disconnected.

My buddy, Paul, who is ahead of me—who is almost always ahead of me on the trail—makes his way back up the hill in response to my yelp. He's a good friend and doesn't laugh until he sees I'm okay. (And, he even waits two whole days to send an e-mail announcing my spill to others in our Bible discussion group. Several guys in our group bike together, but Paul prides himself in being "scar-less," as he puts it. Sudden-onset amnesia has purged his memory of the time he ran into a tree last summer. But, I, along with another mountain bike-scarred friend, Doug, point out later that "scar-less" equals "riskless." Doug suggests that perhaps Paul's bike is not made by Gary Fisher, but *Mary* Fisher. Just part of the "trash talk" that's central to our group's mission statement.)

I gather myself to walk my bike down the rest of the hill. Gun shy. Rock shy. Blood shy. At the top of the hill, it was about mountain biking as a metaphor for a life of faith. You know, the victorious lone believer happily motoring through life. Like the one depicted on the covers of inspirational books, where runners, decked out in cool running gear, circle a track. The life promised in many "gospel" booklets. In other words, the gospel of the neat and tidy.

That was the top of the hill. Here, halfway down the hill—give or take a few yards of sand and rock—that thought had been dislodged from my head. Yeah, mountain biking is a metaphor for the faith journey, but neither of them are a calculated, plotted-out, no-hands coast down a hill. I'm not talking about some loosey-goosey theology, or an undisciplined faith. But I am talking about the mysterious adventure of it all. The Holy Ghost "wild ride" of not quite being in control. Something that's been lost on modern believers with whom it can sometimes seem that God has been examined, dissected, and suspended in formaldehyde.

Halfway down the hill, among the rocks, there is no easy route. No three steps to smooth sailing. You just push through to the end with your compadres, by God, trusting there is an end, a mile or ten miles down the trail. Is it joyless? Hardly. Hardly. Hardly. It has to do with perseverance, faith, community, and the sovereignty of God, rather than ease, comfort, and personal agenda. It has more to do with the reality of faith found in "two-thirds" world countries, probably, than in our culture that has hybridized prosperity and faith, has not experienced persecution, and, as a result, has reveled in comfort.

I'm a product of this culture. With a faith born in ease, I'm much more likely to ask, "Why me, Lord?" than "What's next, Lord?" Thus, my spiritual condition overlaps my biking. Honestly, if my buddies weren't biking through the woods with me, I don't think I'd be here. I've tried it. It's hard work, and the motivation doesn't come easy on my own. Without these companions, I'd be making circles on level blacktop at the neighborhood elementary school. I need a community of people to share

66

the adventure, the stories and the encouragement.

Mountain biking is a metaphor for my faith journey. Community—my small-group buddies—is grace to me. They are a chain link for me to respond to God, to keep going and to persevere, even when I have no idea what God is doing. They are the friends who lower this paralytic through the roof into the presence of Jesus. And, scripture says, "When he saw *their* faith," the paralytic was forgiven and healed. *Their* faith. Community is grace. Mountain biking is grace, too, thank God. And, here, at the bottom of the hill, as we get back on our bikes to crunch down the rest of the trail, I pray the story of the paralytic remains only a spiritual application for me today. Mountain biking is grace.

Funeral for Summer

It's hard to believe she's gone. But, I'm sure I speak for everyone here when I say our lives are better—richer—because she was around. We've laid her out in yellows and oranges and reds. I think that's what she would have wanted. Let everyone take one last long look.

When Summer was here, do you remember how we would spend all day on the beach in Egg Harbor, after breakfast at the Village Café? Digging holes and making monuments and castles with the white rocks. Trying to hold back the Green Bay part of Lake Michigan. And, afterwards, the kids buried each other in that sand. We reclined in the cool water and shuddered upon slipping in for the first time. Some kind of group baptism into a new life of rest. "We pronounce you dead to frantic busyness…" *Dunk! Gasp!* "But, raised to new life," the gulls squawked. Or, at least raised to a few moments of sticking our heads above water and breathing deep. In the name of the Father, and of the Son, and of the Holy Ghost, I threw my keys, and my watch, and my calendar in a drawer and lost track of them for that week in Door County. Amen.

It seems like only yesterday, but when Summer was here, we all sat on that screened-in porch every night after dinner. The stars spilled out across the ink darkness. The moon rose again over the bluff. The Green Bay breezes awakened the beach towels and swimsuits on the makeshift clothesline. The perfect time to try Le Faux Frog, yet another bad bottle of red wine we'd never heard of. And, outside in the yellow porch light glow, under the pines, niece and nephews performed an impromptu talent show. A hip-hop theatre of the absurd. Each act disintegrated into elementary kid snorting and falling down. Cirque Du So-Lame. Then, that stray bat dive-bombed the stage. A scream. The curtain fell. And, the kids tumbled onto the porch for their reviews.

"Great choreography, but lacked passion," my brother said.

"Creative, but needed a stronger finish," their grandmother said.

"I don't get it," my sister said.

But, in the end, "Poignant. Riveting. Delightfully low-brow," *The Chronicle* reported. Because of Summer, and because of that porch, I remembered how much I like all of you. And, wondered why we see each other so little the rest of the year. Life is so short.

Today, we commit Summer to the leaf pile and a good autumn wind. Ashes to ashes, and dust to dust. But there is no need for tears, because we have the hope of resurrection. That, as surely as Winter is coming, Spring will follow. Don't be discouraged. Was it Pascal who said: "What is harder to believe, that something that was alive at one time could come alive again? Or, that something that never was could be in the first place?" Yes. Something like that. Now is the time to practice hope, brothers and sisters.

God rest our beautiful Summer. Amen. And, amen.

Please join us for a coffee and egg salad sandwich luncheon after the service. In lieu of flowers, gifts of beach towels and Le Faux Frog can be left on the front porch. Go in peace.

END NOTES

WINTER

The Dead, of Winter
In northern Illinois, school kids get Casimir Pulaski Day off. No one in Illinois knows who he was. In my hometown of Stevens Point, Wisconsin, there is a statue of Casimir Pulaski. Kids don't get the day off there.

Wisconsin is Grace
First appeared in the arts paper, the *Door Peninsula Voice*, vol. 9, no. 6, March/April 2005. I think we actually called Polish sausage "kielbasa" growing up. They are one and the same. Perhaps in being away from home, one realizes how much he or she has been shaped by it. We are not as different from our roots as maybe we thought or hoped. Maybe we are one and the same.

Speed Bumps for Glaciers
This was written at Leroy's Water Street Café in Ephraim. A warm, rustic coffee place. Makes one want to write, or read, or stare out the window to Eagle Harbor.

December 19
One of our friend's daughters forgot that she'd stopped believing in Santa Claus at Christmas the year before. I laughed because it was so beautiful. That's a sign of grace. A hope for innocence restored.

Tube Socks
The "details count" quote is from author Joni Eareckson-Tada, September 6, 2003 from www.joniandfriends.org.

Tube socks are those long, white athletic socks with two stripes at the top. Certain colored stripes were prized over others. Blue, green, and black were good. Yellow and red were worn only if all others were dirty. Sometimes not even then. There was a year that Grandma White got me something besides tube socks. I thought it was a sign of the second coming of Christ. The gift? A 12" Darth Vader action figure. The next year we were back to tube socks.

The Branches Will Fall Down
The plight of the imposter. I fear that my cover will be blown. But what if it isn't a cover?

The Wisconsin & Illinois Truce of '07
An update: My friend, Wendell, was telling the truth about Wisconsin's southern border. I knew it! You can find out more about this in the book *How the States Got Their Shapes* by Mark Stein (Smithsonian, 2008).

Emmaus Road
The gospel of Luke, chapter 24.

SPRING

Thaw
First appeared in the arts paper, *Peninsula Pulse*, vol. 13, no. 22, October 5, 2007.

Harbors & Boat Launches
Appeared in the *Door Peninsula Voice*, vol. 10, no. 2, July/August 2005.

Indigenous Animals
This appeared in the August 1, 2008 issue of the *Peninsula Pulse*, as an Honorable Mention in the Hal Grutzmacher Writer's Expose.

Aldo Leopold's Warning
First appeared in the *Peninsula Pulse*, December 2007. Read Leopold's *A Sand County Almanac* (Oxford Press) first published in 1949. Read it in the woods. You must also, if you can, dig up the music of Mark Heard. He died in 1992, at the age of forty. I was at the show where he had the heart attack that lead to his death a month later. Try to find a copy of *Second Hand* (Fingerprint Records, 1991) and *Dry Bones Dance* (1990). Americana with insightful poetry. You can read Willimon's article, "The God We Hardly Knew," in the *Christian Century*, December 21-28, 1988.

SUMMER

Adeste Fideles
Adeste Fideles: Latin. Literally: "Approach, or be present, faithful ones." Or, as the Christmas carol bids us: "O Come, All Ye Faithful." The short story, "The Living," appears in *The Annie Dillard Reader* (HarperCollins, 1994, 1995). Haven't read her? I humbly suggest starting

with *Teaching a Stone to Talk: Expeditions & Encounters* (HarperCollins, 1982).

FALL

To Whom It May Concern
Written on the porch of the historic Alpine Resort in Egg Harbor, on a rainy, sixty-three degree day in July. I wrote this as a piece for a seasonal show I do with my musician friends, Greg and Kim Wheaton.

Hunting for Words
This was written at the Drink Coffee cafe in Sister Bay. Good coffee, good baked items, in this tucked-away spot. Read August Derleth's *The Wisconsin: River of a Thousand Isles* (University of Wisconsin Press, 1985) for a strange and wonderful history of the Wisconsin River. "Hunting for Words" first appeared in the *Peninsula Pulse*, vol. 13, no. 26, November 2-16, 2007. My hunt for words has been greatly aided by the writer's group that meets monthly at my church. They are a nice group of people, but not too nice.

Raising Ebenezers
This essay appeared in the *Door Peninsula Voice*, vol. 10, no. 4, Winter 2005-2006. The Terry Scott Taylor penned song, "Ordinary Extraordinary Day," mentioned here is from the album, *Mr. Buechner's Dream* (Stunt Records, 2001) by the band Daniel Amos. The recording is a tribute to writer Frederick Buechner. *Listening to Your Life* (Harper, 1992), with its daily readings is a condensed, reflective place to start.

Coming Late
After growing up with the idea that alcohol and religion don't mix, it's ironic that I spend every other week with a group of guys at PJ's Courthouse Tap to discuss God over a few brews. I don't think he minds. Leinie's Creamy Dark tops my list.

Mock Chicken Legs
Good luck finding ground veal for this recipe. I went to three stores and a meat market and still never found it. I just doubled the amount of pork. My wife and kids were gracious in trying these for dinner one night, although they were not too sure. My daughter said, "I'm really not hungry." To which my son replied, "You're just trying to get out of it."

And my funny wife chimed in, "Maybe we should take them over to our neighbor who is recovering from knee surgery. To be neighborly." But, in the end we agreed they were just OK. Not exactly like the ones we used to get from the Piggly Wiggly. And, further, we agreed they needed a better name. Suggestions included: "meatball-on-a-stick," "popsicle burger," and our daughter's "owl pellet-on-a-stick." My suggestion is to skip the recipe entirely, and try and find some pre-made at The Pig.

Postcards from the Edge of the Bluff
I lied. There is one good fish fry in Illinois: Captain Vic's Fish & Seafood Market in Sycamore, Illinois. All-you-can-eat haddock on Tuesdays and Fridays.

Mountain Biking is Grace
Student Leadership Journal, Winter/Spring 2004. The beautiful story of the paralytic appears in the gospels of Mark 2:1-12 and Luke 5:17-26.

Funeral for Summer
First appeared in the arts paper *Peninsula Pulse,* vol. 13, no. 24, October 19, 2007.

Cornerstone Press

CEO	Dan Dieterich
President	Kyle Bernander
Corporate secretary	Jeremy Larsen
Editor-in-chief	Lauren Shimulunas
Publicity director	Kacie Otto
Publicity co-director	Tracy Berg
Business manager	Krystle Fandrey
Fulfillment manager	Ty Natzke
Advertising manager	Katelynn Paape
Marketing manager	Melinda McCord
Sales manager	Amy VanMeter
Managing editor	Andrew Stepan
Head copy editor	Amanda Waddington
- Associates	Philecia Pribnow
	Emily Fish
	Ty Natzke
Head substance editor	Lee Wickman
- Associates	Eric Rueth
	Allison Herr
	Tanner Hoffman
	John Leonhardt
Production manager	Erin Mueller
Production co-manager	Mara Thiel
Webmaster	Falan Shulfer
Book Designer	Scott Gerstl